Ermm...
WORDS FOR WHEN YOU ARE LOST FOR WORDS

Franz Pagot

THE PERFECT *P* EDITION

www.theperfectedition.com

First published in United Kingdom
by The Perfect Edition in 2015
copyright © 2015 Franz Pagot
The moral right of the author has been asserted.

ISBN code: 9780957650091

The Perfect Edition
Communications House 26 York Street
London W1U 6PZ United Kingdom
info@theperfectedition.com
www.theperfectedition.com

Illustrations by Franz Pagot

To Enrico and Elena,
no more words of advice, but words
that can advise you.

INDEX

ACKNOWLEDGEMENTS

I have collected many of the words-strings in the following pages whilst in the company of extraordinary people, noting what they do or say.

I have simply penned moments they gave me in order to better acknowledge their unwitting generosity.

First and foremost a deep thank you to my best friend Dave Judge, who displays honesty and generosity along with nonchalant humour - a large quantity of the positive thoughts in this little tome come from working or simply spending time together.

He is such an inspiration that Enrico, my son, always said that when he grew up he wanted to become a 'davejudge'; I wish I became one too.

A big thank you to Richard Bedser, not just a dear friend but also a bright gem of wisdom, I have stolen a few things he said to me and made them my own.

Thank you to Meg Rosoff, successful and famous writer of incredible talent; I wish I could give you answers, but I ran out of words.

Thank you also to all the bad teachers who gave me the best lessons, I have not stolen from them, but I certainly learned what not to take.

And finally, a heartfelt thank-you to my editor, Jo Asker, who performed CPR on many phrases and gave others new and meaningful life.

And thank you, the reader, for having the courage to buy this book; make sure you don't comment as you read, it might be used in my next book!

"It's only words unless they're true."
— *David Mamet*

INTRODUCTION

Will you, the reader, be disappointed?

The very thought kills me...

And who would dare publish a book of his very own aphorisms?

What (or who) made me perform this spooky act of arrogance?

It was the X-Files.

Yes.

That wonderful mystery-shrouded TV series that made us all fall in love with agent Scully and feel sorry for agent Mulder... most of the time.

I was watching an old episode titled "Grotesque" (*episode 14, series III, 1996*) one evening and suddenly agent Mulder spoke my words, the very words I wrote years beforehand, of which very few people knew about:

Special Agent Patterson: "I have to tell you, I'm really disappointed in you."

Mulder: "Well, I wouldn't want to disappoint you by not disappointing you."

I wrote that, even though the writer of that episode, Howard Gordon, couldn't have known.

It was a phrase I used often at the beginning of my career, in the 80s, when most people I worked for were never happy, never satisfied and constantly disappointed.

In fact, it all started even before then, when I was just a kid:

"You disappoint me." I heard from my Judo teacher when I was just 10 years old; I got involved in a fight in the locker rooms and I later refused to give the name of who started it.

I will never forget my Sensei's blazing eyes when he slapped me with those words.

Then it was the turn of my Latin and Greek high school teacher: you disappoint me Pagot, he would say in his cavernous voice, while handing me a very bad mark for my disastrous Greek-to-Latin translation test.

The disappointed look seemed a constant gaze as I grew up, and my parents were no exception...

Thereby, I decided to come up with my own special answer, so I could make people smile:

"I would hate to disappoint you by not disappointing you." Hearing those same words from Mulder's lips made me think it was time to go public, share other words openly, before they ended up yet again echoing someone's dialogue on the screen.

I have made many notes over the years, especially on set, but also while seated in cafes, on trains and even at the dentist - comments overheard while drinking macchiato: flippant remarks made during lovers tiffs, humorous and equally bitter comments as well as gems of wisdom by unsuspecting characters.

I always thought this material would eventually work its way into my next screenplay, finding new life as words spoken by a character I liked, or a villain I created in worlds I imagined.

Being tapped on the shoulder while fiercely arguing with your alter ego can be embarrassing and I was often brought back to reality being stared at by people with a look reserved for madmen.

Tell me you do this too, sometimes.

The following pages contain bits of those dialogues, some of which were told to me directly, like "You are a creased man with no wrinkles", which is how my daughter sees me because of my utter disinterest for my appearance or for perfectly ironed clothes, telling me off frequently because my shirt resembles unfolded origami rather than Armani's finest.

But she never said I disappoint her.

Will I disappoint You then?

My hope is for you to find words here that will aid in filling empty silences here and there, replacing those three dots that plague conversations so much.

I even hope to make you smile to yourself, perhaps cause the odd chuckle.

If you find some of these aphorisms elsewhere, please let me know, and especially do let me know if some are identical to yours. I promise I did not steal from you, but console yourself that great minds think alike (someone famous and clever said that!).

Lastly, you will not find the following sentences ordered into categories, even though quite a few people asked me to do so; sorting out phrases by theme robs the reader of an element of surprise, they are best read casually, wildly even, starting cheekily from the last page (I know you do that).

I hope you will not be disappointed, because *this* time I really would hate to disappoint you by disappointing you.

Little did I know that this was the big question.

CHAPTER ONE
(and only)

1 You disappoint me, she said. I would hate to disappoint you by not disappointing you, was the answer.

2 I lie so I feel less liable.

3 If I choose not to choose, isn't that a choice?

4 I have so much metal in me that when I die, my body will not go to science but to a scrap yard.

5   I keep fit so it's easier to chase my dreams.

6   Little did I know that this was the big question.

7   Every time he gives me a hug I have the impression he is just checking the best spot to stab me in the back.

8   I always listen carefully to what is not said.

9   Black and white is good for the grey matter.

10 I'd rather fail miserably because I tried than be miserable because I didn't.

11 I am tired of having to reinvent myself.

12 I have never experienced something clever on the tip of my tongue, but I have surely produced plenty of well spelled out stupidities.

13 You are the best not when you look good but when you make everyone else look good.

14 I often have brilliant thoughts I disagree with.

15 I always question someone who has all the answers.

16 I write things I have no memory of but that I can recall perfectly in my mind.

17 I am a creased man with no wrinkles.

18 I am not an insomniac: I just haven't finished thinking.

19 I have met some geniuses and I was misunderstood.

20 Don't keep your past closer than your future.

Elegance can be cheated, style never can be.

21 The most beautiful things arrive without drums rolling, without even a whisper.

22 Be prepared to accept criticism and listen to others who have done it *differently*, not necessarily better.

23 Elegance can be cheated, style never can be.

24 I scored badly at my urine test, never mind my IQ's.

25 It's easy to be modest when we have done nothing, and easy to be arrogant if we haven't done enough.

26 I was born in Conegliano, a small town in Italy. I didn't have a choice.

27 Certainty in life? I doubt it.

28 Don't open a door to enter into the world, open it to let the world in.

29 Some people are terribly apt at turning a solution into a problem.

30 I don't feel lonely when I am on my own; I have plenty of things I can argue about with myself.

31 My parents never understood me as a teenager but they read me quite well since my father used to slap me on the back of my head every evening - he was sure I'd done something. Boy was he right!

32 You don't know what to say? Don't worry, I am sure you'll come up with something stupid.

33 What am I supposed to say to that? I'll tell you what... I'll just ad-lib.

34 The fact that nobody understands you doesn't make you an artist.

35 Other people's stupidity is less uncomfortable than my own.

36 Books have chapters so an author can see where the words go and hide.

37 We understand a person better only once we start remembering them.

38 I hope to never be found dead in an embarrassing position.

39 I'm no fatalist; I just can't avoid what happens to me.

40 She has an answer even when she doesn't understand the question.

An exclamation mark often covers up a question.

41 If you are struggling to explain it, it's probably not worthy of comprehension.

42 Intimacy is lost at the first fart.

43 An exclamation mark often covers up a question.

44 Sometimes we put a full stop where there should be a comma instead.

45 A good father doesn't need to be at home, but he should be present.

46 My life needs editing, I have far too much material.

47 Television is now reaching its lowest levels of mediocrity.

48 He is like turquoise, neither blue nor green.

49 Don't try to impress me with your talent, scare
me with it.

50 I wanted to live like an artist, but the art just
dried up.

51 Some people don't live badly; they're just bad at
living.

52 Does *it's the thought that counts* indicate that you
are a mean and thoughtless bastard?

53 Crossing a line you did not draw cannot be bad.

54 You don't have to understand the rules to break
them, but you had better fully understand the
consequences.

55 It's fine to have a *strong* ego, but keep it small.

56 The more I understand, the more I doubt.

57 Going down a hot metal slide with bare buttocks wasn't the worse trauma I experienced as a child.

58 Our pain is a silent scream when hurt in front of others laughing at us.

59 Rather than a monologue from her, I prefer a dialogue with myself.

60 He asks for my friendship on Facebook, likes everything I post on Instagram and follows me on Twitter, yet barely says Hi when he sees me.

61 He thinks the only time he's wrong is when he doubts himself.

I see dead people and they have a great life.

62 I like you as you are (but could you change a little?).

63 When in doubt I buy two of each, just in case.

64 We agreed on the fact that we disagree on everything.

65 I see dead people and they have a great life.

66 When people cannot argue back they always say you are crazy.

67 If a couple no longer get along, it's neither his fault nor hers; it's the relationship's fault.

68 Happiness? Looking for it makes me sad.

69 Time heals all wounds after rubbing them in alcohol.

70 You don't have to get pregnant to become a good gynaecologist and you don't have to kill someone to write a murder novel.

71 There is no such thing as a friend, only true friends or people you know better than others.

72 He is such a conman that he changed his name to be able to live with himself.

73 An honest arrogance is easier to digest than a false modesty.

74 I am not upset with you but I cherish the moment I will never see you again.

75 Why do mathematicians want to square the circle? Would you swing a picture frame instead of a hula-hoop around your hips?

76 It scares me when someone tells me not to be scared.

77 He is so in love with himself that he talks to strangers who wear mirrored glasses.

78 Don't sit on the toilet with your phone in the back pocket.

79 I won't retire: I will just expire.

80 I hope you believe in Karma, because mine is an unpaid and thankless job.

81 Never mind flying pigs, I no longer see angels.

82 Love is the only sentiment that can improve anything.

83 Learning invaluable skills makes you worth it.

I was born in the evening and have been chasing light ever since.

84 An unsolicited manuscript doesn't know proper manners.

85 When someone tells you what's good *and* what is bad for you, it's not good.

86 I was born in the evening and have been chasing light ever since.

87 Tying yourself up on your own is really not a good idea.

88 I am happy to laugh at myself anytime but not ready to be the joke.

89 My writing is only a bookmark of a bigger and better book.

90 Old equipment is better than no equipment.

91 I was born in Italy and learned pretty quickly not to sit next to the window in restaurants, never to argue with a waiter, upset the local cop or disrespect Mum. The latter was the most dangerous.

92 Don't look down to the water if you have your phone in the top pocket.

93 Good at nothing is better than no good at all.

94 Every time I kissed her I felt like I was water from the sky turning into rain.

95 Take your work seriously but be prepared to laugh at yourself. If you can't, I will.

96 I am not overweight, there is just more of me to love.

97 She was so elegant and light that she left no prints in the sand.

98 If you keep preparing you will never be ready.

99 I prefer to follow the instinct of a woman more than the confidence of a man.

100 I spend so much time thinking that some-times I end up with butt ache.

101 One of those faces you see once and easily forget.

102 I am a love veteran.

103 When there is nothing to laugh at, being serious is the only possible humour.

104 I fear not being scared anymore.

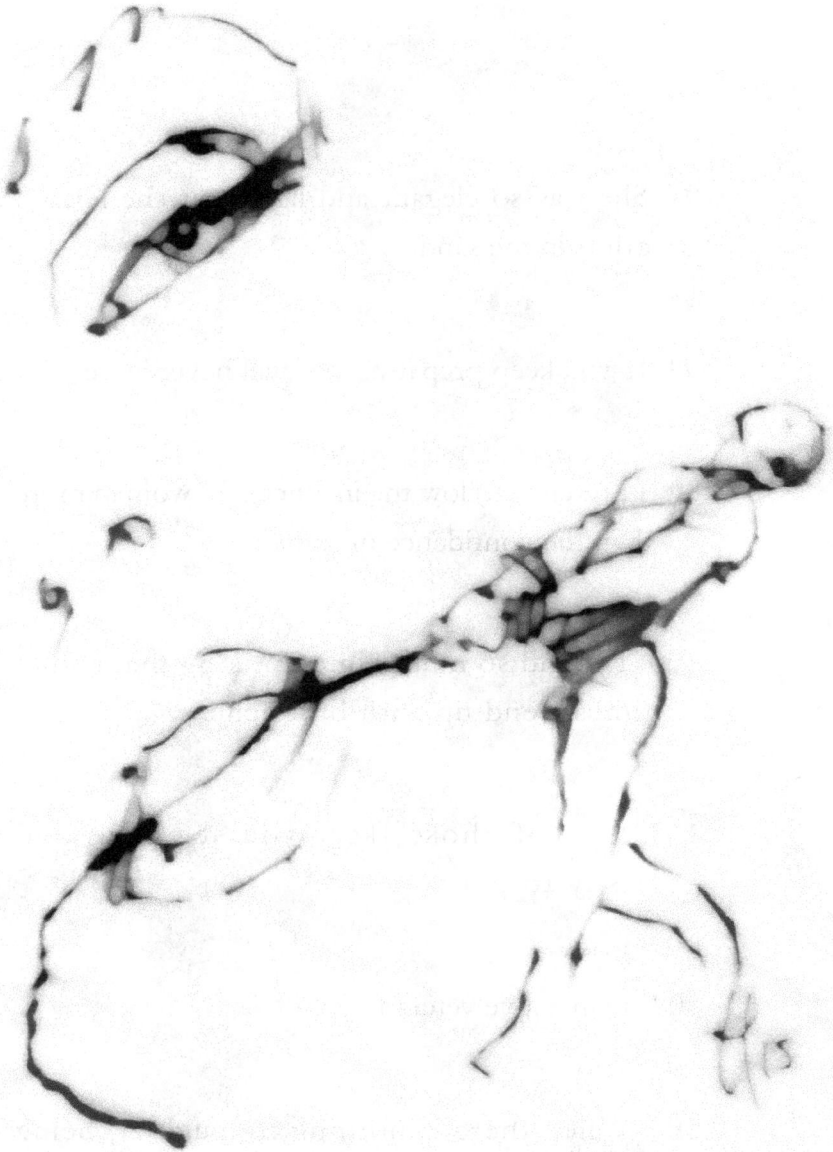

Great love always starts with a threat: I want to be with you forever.

105 Helpless at being able not to help yourself means you are a kleptomaniac.

106 Stupities are stupidities that stupefy.

107 I work hard and play hard, just not sure what the game is anymore.

108 Great love always starts with a threat: I want to be with you forever.

109 Live what you are supposed to live without thinking what you are supposed to do.

110 'Never' has a timeless quality to it: I use it all the time.

111 Mankind and *humanity* don't fit some people I have met.

112　There is no point arguing with him, it's a bit like attempting synchronised swimming in a force ten gale.

113　I am useless with diplomacy, because I cannot stoop to compromises.

114　We could live forever if we had no memory.

115　Advertising will sell you the most useless, ugly and expensive product if the message is loud and frequent enough.

116　All I can give you for sure is a definite maybe.

117　Being in love, it's not the years that matter but the minutes - unless you are madly in love, then every second counts.

118　I also dream other people's dreams.

119 The whole point of advertising is to make you feel bad. Bad about yourself, your laundry, your car, your husband; not that you need an ad to know about the latter.

120 Everyone says you should live and let live but they should live and let *dream*.

121 I do not like groups, parties, and associations, for their unified voice is easily manipulated or distorted. Compare the strength of thousands of separate yet identical opinions

122 I am not interested in knowing certain people better; I despise them enough already.

123 The moment someone says to me that I am part of the team, I feel very lonely.

124 Find silence if you want to hear the answers you are asking of yourself.

I don't write, I merely describe what I see.

125 I am not a pessimist, just a dreamer with my feet deep in the shit.

126 My memories cloud my future.

127 I would share my solitude with my best friend if I had one.

128 I don't write, I merely describe what I see.

129 I think you should trade your reality for someone's imagination.

130 I don't like sad endings and despise happy endings. I prefer the right ending, as every ending should be.

131 They sweat for hours in the gym but yet take the lift when they leave.

132 Forgetting *something* is bad; forgetting *someone* is cruel.

133 If you don't like my answer, want to try rephrasing the question?

134 I'd rather have people thinking I am a fool because I asked rather than think I am fool because I did not know.

135 I would love to experience boredom, but I am way too busy.

136 I hate it when someone says that they are speechless and then hit you with a wordy tsunami.

137 A job for life sounds much less heroic than a life of work.

138 If you want to progress in your job never commit yourself to anything unless you're a freelancer, because people will think you are lazy and incompetent.

139 Some people get up before they fall.

140 The best advice I received for working successfully behind the camera is to wear comfortable shoes.

141 If you think a picture is worth a thousand words you haven't been to the same art galleries I have.

142 I prefer to watch paint peeling over watching a Power Point presentation.

143 Nuns raised me. They taught me everything bad I know and everything bad there was to know.

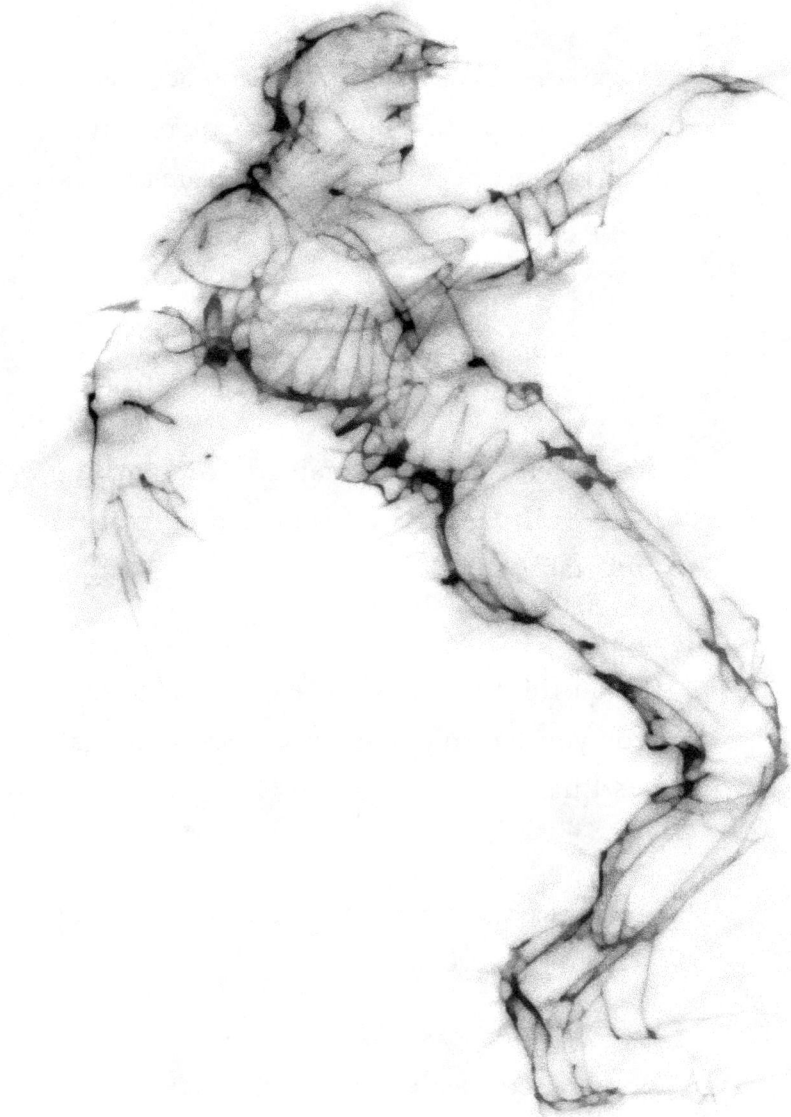

My body is not a temple but a battleground.

144 The most hopelessly idiotic phrases are always about hope.

145 At the end of the day, it's just another day.

146 She talks all the time to hide thoughts she does not have.

147 My body is not a temple but a battleground.

148 It was perfectly clear until he gave me an example.

149 If you disagree with me it proves my point.

150 The only currency that works anywhere and with anyone: respect. You can "pay" respect but you cannot buy it, it's given to you, but not for free; once gained, easily lost and once lost, you cannot get more.

151 A true friend doesn't say "I haven't seen you for such a long time" but instead "You haven't changed!".

152 You will fall sooner or later, just don't cry … and get up!

153 Move on and turn another page they say. But what if I *started* at the last page?

154 I dipped my toes in the sea for the first time - one small step towards drowning.

155 Jump without looking? Are you mad? I could hit the ceiling!

156 Living in hope is in fact only procrastinating about certainty.

157 A smile can hide something, tears cannot.

158 Free your mind. Be free. Impossible is nothing. But before you do that, buy the shoes. Just do it.

159 A true friend will not tell you off, but instead offer a solution first, and then tell you off.

160 Stop looking for the meaning of life and give your life some sense.

161 She pouted in a way that only her mum could love.

162 All good things must come to an end, but when do they start?

163 I reached an age when I realised I'll never read all the books I own.

164 The more you dream the more you are free.

You are seldom what you think you are, because it is rarely what you think it is.

42

165 We should visit people before visiting amazing buildings or grand monuments; even mountains will come to us, but people will be gone if we wait too long.

166 Do I believe in life after death? Hell no.

167 You are seldom what you think you are because it is rarely what you think it is.

168 I've been in places where ten minutes felt like a lifetime.

169 I know it's a problem, but it's not my problem; it's your problem. Is that a problem?

170 It's a slippery slope and someone is greasing it all up.

171 God created heaven; man keeps creating hell.

172 I have bought terrible music because I liked the cover.

173 The way they picture heaven is my idea of hell.

174 Love is an abstraction in search of physical confirmation.

175 Men lie to get something, women lie to protect someone.

176 You are proportionally richer the less you have.

177 If you knew him like I do you wouldn't want to know him at all.

178 We worry that one day, artificial intelligence will destroy mankind; no need to worry about that, our natural stupidity is already speeding that up.

179 My thoughts sometimes resemble a time-lapse sequence: fast, blurry and full of striking lights.

180 To understand one person you should love many.

181 A writer in the computer age is often lost in Word.

182 Superman stops bullets with his teeth and spits them back, and that is clearly a superiority complex.

183 Life should be lived, not told.

184 I don't stay awake asking myself questions nor do I not sleep because I am pondering the answers.

185 Nothing is stupid if said with love.

I don't mind a quick kiss, if it lasts long enough.

186 We can't all be poets, but we can look for poetry in everything we do.

187 I don't mind a quick kiss, if it lasts long enough.

188 I don't resent the dreams that never happen; I just dream some more.

189 Don't fade on me, it's bad editing.

190 There are moments when I feel a desperate need to collect myself, not just pick myself up.

191 Fight for what you believe in. You may lose, but you'll feel great.

192 The only nights I cannot forget are the ones I could not sleep.

193 The most dangerous liar is the sincere one; the one who truly believes his own lies.

194 I used to go for a run or hit the punch bag on a bad day, nowadays I do some housework and put adrenaline to good use.

195 He looked like the kind of guy who shoots first and asks questions later.

196 Of course I watch TV, but I never turn it on.

197 The most beautiful monuments reflect an inner fear.

198 So many people trying to get a job - if only they'd do some work it would be a good start.

199 Politicians answer in such a way that one starts questioning the question.

200 I have never done anything in alphabetical order; in fact I have never arranged anything in any order at all. I believe in orderly chaos.

201 Love is like bread; it either goes stale with time or you are left with crumbs.

202 Intuition is not creativity until it finds execution.

203 It's the same worms, no matter how many times I open the can.

204 I hate explaining why I've been out of touch for so long, so I stay out of touch even longer.

205 I use words like a blanket when it's cold, pulling it over my head, giving me comfort.

206 He walked away to make a point and make us feel at a loss. We didn't.

She would enter a room and time wouldn't just stand still, it would screech to a halt.

207 It's still a terrible film, doesn't matter on how many 'D's' it was shot on. *(Referring to 3-D)*

208 The moment he had to go straight, he was a zigzag man.

209 She would enter a room and time wouldn't just stand still, it would screech to a halt.

210 The only way to talk to her is to write slowly.

211 You cannot step forward without changing your balance.

212 The sea is like an open invitation without a dress code.

213 He cannot plan anything, just look at his last ten relationships.

214 Slow? I have seen glaciers moving faster than him!

215 A face that has seen things we don't want to know about.

216 I don't think it was your fault, but I am in a minority.

217 I don't know what to say, he said. Great, that saves us a conversation, she answered.

218 She is like a giraffe: her brain well away from her heart.

219 The moment someone said to you 'Take your seat' you lost your freedom.

220 I never felt special or different from others; I could never do that to myself.

221 He is my rock. All he does is lay motionless.

222 True, everything has been done before, but that doesn't mean it must be presented in the same way.

223 Writing is admitting that you are not happy.

224 If the truth is in the middle, where lies the lie?

225 She speaks so much and so fast that bullets, in comparison, exit machine guns like people exiting a funeral.

226 Some action films feel like dressing on a salad: a strange aftertaste after swallowing wimpy stuff.

227 I no longer hate her, but I forget her constantly.

Going after some ideas can be the last place you'll ever go.

228 The most important thing when it comes to sex is foreplay; the secret is in the word 'play'.

229 New operating systems rarely operate as they ought to - often they just sit there on the desktop, being fabulous.

230 Going after some ideas can be the last place you'll ever go.

231 Lying and breathing for some people are the same thing: unconditional reflexes.

232 A substitute for love? The memory of it.

233 He fancies himself as an actor so much that he has this "fuck me sideways" grin.

234 Beauty comes from within, unless your x-rays say otherwise.

235 She is so loud that your fillings would jar in your teeth.

236 'I don't know' - the bravest thing anyone can say.

237 When she left him the house was so empty that there wasn't even a mouse under the floorboards.

238 No brain and no shame: spooky combination.

239 Some good people die badly - it rarely happens the other way round.

240 It was easier to revolt when despots lived in palaces.

241 I can do without life's essentials, providing I have its luxuries.

242 He likes the smell of his own bullshit, like not minding your own farts yet detesting others.

243 Her words were dancing on air, like hippos on heat.

244 I am not thinking at the moment, just rearranging the future in my head.

245 A firm decision should always be taken in the greatest of uncertainties.

246 Doesn't matter how physically close he was, we were still miles away.

247 She was the kind of person who knew answers to questions that people never ask.

248 Why must I look at reality? Isn't a glance every now and then enough?

She has a mind of her own, and a body to match.

249 Beautiful theories are often spoilt by ugly facts.

250 Which version do you want? The quick and the ugly ok?

251 She has a mind of her own, and a body to match.

252 While some people look at pixels and resolution, I make images and create emotions.

253 If that means you being in your right mind, I hope you go insane.

254 Keep trying; eventually one of the keys will work.

255 I haven't written anything decent today, not enough suffering.

256 He's a piece of art and should be hanging in a museum. In fact, he should just be hanging.

257 I have a very bad memory; I remember what I try to forget.

258 Flowers grow and blossom from dirt, not gold.

259 The more I wonder with my brain the more I wander with my feet.

260 I take pictures so I can see things.

261 You know you love someone when you hear your own voice saying things you would normally never say.

262 We hug those we love so we can feel whole again.

263 Move on, but keep your mistakes around so they can still reproach you.

264 I would love to change my life, but the guarantee expired a while ago.

265 The less a movie is understood the more it is praised.

266 I was told not to miss the boat but it turned out that the lake froze.

267 I know there's no 'but' - I was just contemplating the 'ifs'.

268 Some people discuss the needs of the man in the street, and then leave their high-rise offices in a limousine, to reach their private jet.

What if the right direction is the one taken by salmon?

269 I haven't written anything today, I am in between ideas.

270 Some people make little sense, regardless of what they're saying.

271 What if the right direction is the one taken by salmon?

272 A kiss is synchronised breathing.

273 Sometimes I think about disappearing, then I realise that nobody truly notices me anyway.

274 Do you like it? She prompted. I guess I'll have to get used to it, was the answer.

275 Sadly, shit floats instead of sinking.

276 I doubt that to say 'I love you' constantly, is anything else but a reminder to yourself.

277 Some people have that dead look in their eyes like the only thing they live for is to get through the day.

278 Maybe the best way to help someone is to hide your own experience.

279 I have wonder in my brain and wander in my blood.

280 He is so good at what he does that he turns professionals into amateurs.

281 It was as much fun as playing with an underground train model set.

282 Beauty happens when standards are broken.

283 Good writers for children choose simple words not because a child can understand better, but because it's parents who will have to read them hundreds of times.

284 Racists are on the wrong side of history.

285 The weaker we are the more inventive we become.

286 If you want to find a *real* man stop looking so *fake*.

287 My mother always said I loved playing with sunlight in my cot. I think my parents were trying to blind me.

288 'I only wish I could have stayed longer' never comes to mind whilst there.

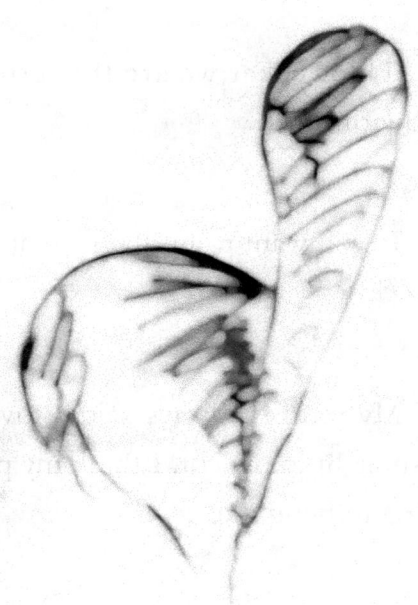

I left my heart on her lips.

289 It's not bad, just worse than the worst-case scenario!

290 People in love are the best - always late, clumsy and careless, often absent.

291 I left my heart on her lips.

292 You cannot be focused and be in love. Love is a beautiful distraction.

293 Light does not need anyone. Like darkness.

294 I understand him perfectly when he says nothing.

295 Actors wear a face hoping that such a mask will transform them into divas.

296 I gave my best to some of the worst people.

297 Some people speak many languages yet have nothing worthy to say.

298 I never fancied men sexually; I already had enough problems with women.

299 I was always too young and then suddenly discovered I was too old.

300 I have seen hell and found it vastly underrated.

301 Put some thought to that, but leave your brain out.

302 Less is more, more or less, and sometimes less is a bore.

303 The sky is the limit they say. Unless it's raining.

304 When I write, the sheet of paper is waiting for me, white with fear.

305 I missed the boat because I was waiting on the wrong pier.

306 To err is human; to persevere is also human.

307 Filmmaking is a collaborative business where everyone has the same goal: cancel what everyone else does better than you.

308 A boring person makes you waste time you do not have.

309 Deeds are often short of words.

310 Each of us is a work of art. Finding the right audience who will appreciate how valuable we are is a different matter.

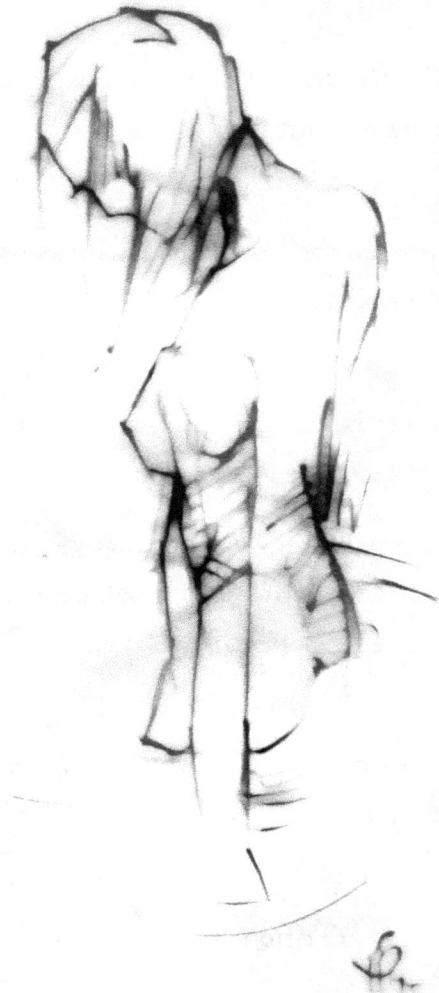

I'd rather have very clear feelings than very clear ideas.

311 More frightening than going forwards is staying still.

312 Loving her is like a natural reflex.

313 I'd rather have very clear feelings than very clear ideas.

314 You know when you have found a great writer when he makes you feel clever reading his books.

315 I let reality fade at times, just enough to stay bright.

316 I normally work harder when I am out of work.

317 Doesn't matter how far you go, it's the impression you leave that counts.

318 True I have no regrets, except regretting having none.

319 I want to make moving images that move people.

320 Reality is a distraction to my fantasies.

321 He has no charisma: only McDonald's takes his orders.

322 If our fate is already written, why can't we read it? Who is the publisher?

323 We worry so much about our future and we forget to enjoy our present.

324 While worrying about the staircase we stand at the bottom of the stairs instead of climbing the first step.

325 Running out of excuses is the worst excuse.

326 The problem with Italians in the creative business is that they all fancy themselves as Da Vinci's semen.

327 I am happy, but sadly aware of it.

328 Believe me when I say don't believe in anything.

329 Some people are keen to put me in a pigeon-hole along with their notes.

330 I was born a veteran.

331 How can you expect her to understand what you say when you don't acknowledge her silence?

332 People's perception of fair-trade is often far from fair.

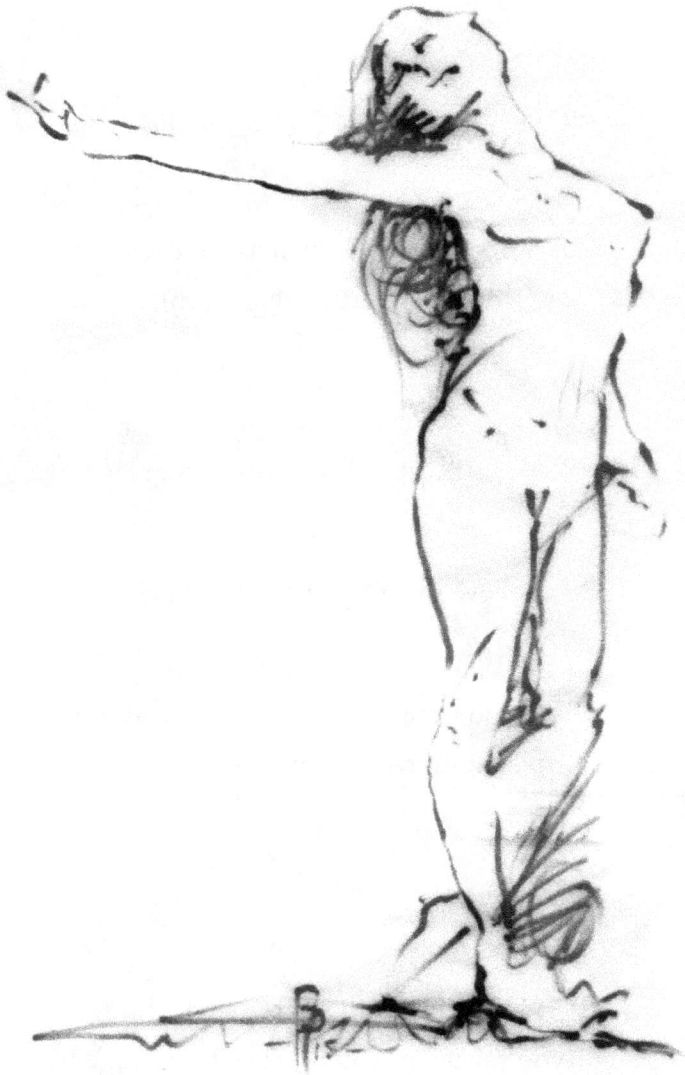

Stay close to me; I am your lucky charm.

74

333 Never pronounce words you are not comfortable with, your lips will be embarrassed.

334 What I truly enjoy of any activity is not the end
but the beginning; that is exciting!

335 Stay close to me; I am your lucky charm.

336 People we love the most are not beautiful, they are precious.

337 Nowadays people are used, and things are
loved - it should be the other way around.

338 'Do you remember when' is a phrase that will
encourage tears.

339 People who generally detest me are the ones
who individually congratulate me the most.

340 If you keep quiet when in a minority they will make you a minority.

341 Once we lose the sense of wonder we acquire yawns and groans.

342 I don't know what a masterpiece is but I sure know when something is original.

343 He speaks sentences that make no sense but are grammatically correct.

344 People create traditions, though traditions do not make a person.

345 Lie to me, I don't mind. Tell me how handsome and clever I am.

346 To feel is the most beautiful thing, there is no intent, you do it or you don't.

347 Sorry, it didn't cross my mind, because it was already on my mind.

348 The only way to deal with the future is to face the past.

349 The best inventions came from being too lazy.

350 There are people I want to kill because they are such a waste of time, yet others I love killing time with.

351 Worse than someone asking too many questions is someone asking questions *and* giving the answers.

352 Open your heart but mind the draught.

353 We pay for our choices even when we have no choice at all.

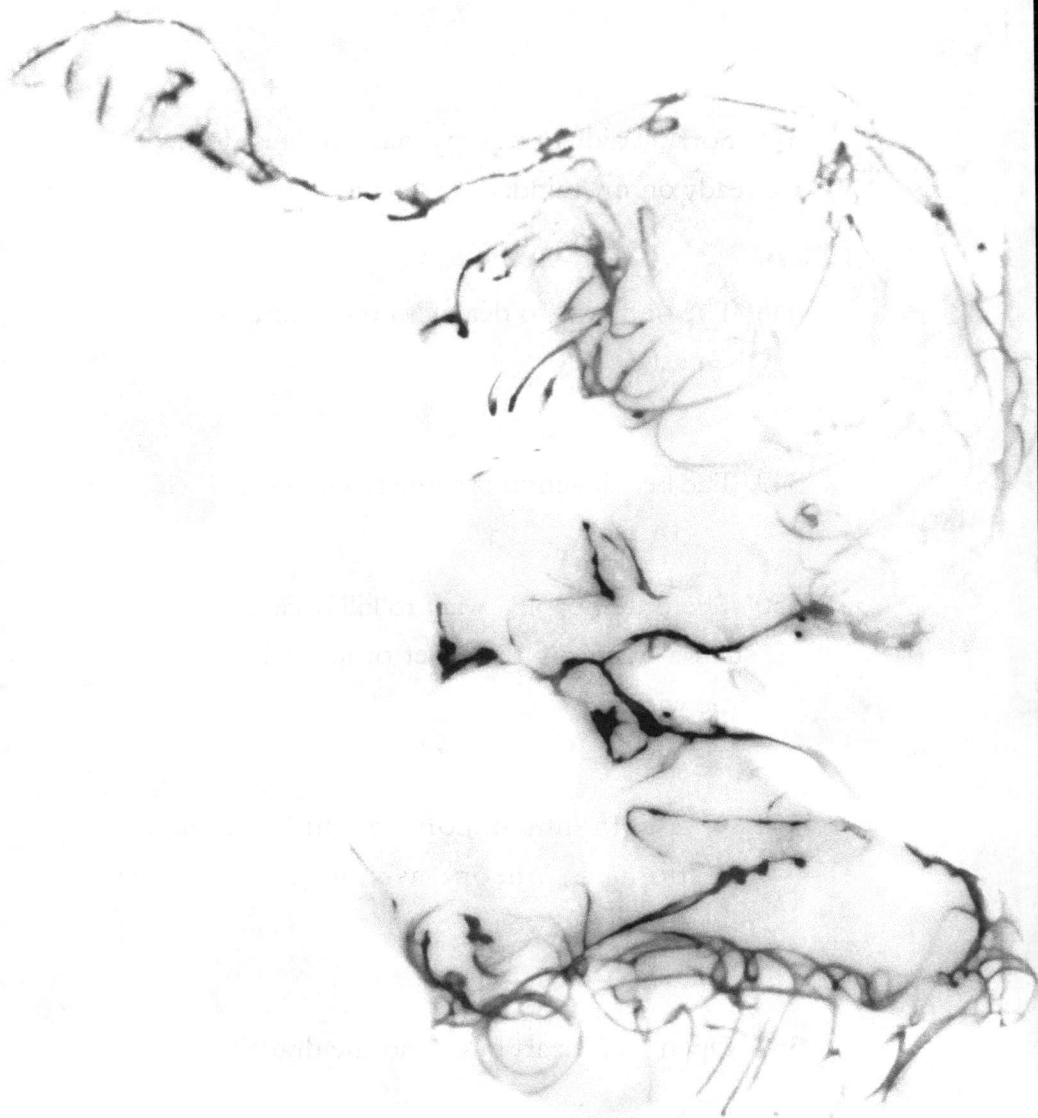

So many phrases about the meaning of a kiss, when all that matters is a kiss with meaning.

354 It was the most difficult time of my life, yet I felt incredibly happy, like a madman in an asylum.

355 So many phrases about the meaning of a kiss, when all that matters is a kiss with meaning.

356 I never tried to be a better person but I constantly try to make others feel better.

357 The more I tell the truth, the more they think I am lying.

358 I'd rather admit that I have had, than recognise what I should have had.

359 These days, media, not government, shapes a country.

360 He has such a bad memory that he always agrees with anyone, even when he disagrees.

361 There is a limit to what we can enjoy, dictated by how much we can love.

362 A bitter person is someone who cannot forgive others when realising he did not achieve his goal.

363 I have been stabbed in the back so many times that when someone taps my shoulder I am already bleeding.

364 I started to feel certain of my choices the moment all my certainties fell apart.

365 I don't like looking back, I get distracted and hurt myself each time I do that.

366 He was so irritating because he was so similar to me.

367 We talked empty words; we gave no sense to phrases, yet we understood each other perfectly.

368 Doesn't matter how hard I try, I can only be me.

369 I am happy *behind* the camera; I couldn't bear watching any of my own actions in playback.

370 No point of sound advice amongst the deaf.

371 Are you sure this is a problem? Or is the problem the fact you are considering this a problem?

I kiss with my eyes open because I cannot believe it's happening.

82

372 The dark is only a question of light.

373 The past is not a comfortable place to be for too long.

374 I kiss with my eyes open because I cannot believe it's happening.

375 I am trying to get old without growing up.

376 My plan is simple: we steal happiness, run away and once safe we divide it in half. Deal?

377 I never contemplated suicide; the thought of getting it wrong kills me.

378 People don't change, we do.

379 The biggest mistake is not the mistake itself but what we do with it.

380 We loved each other with so much passion that we were on fire, and I saved her every time from burning.

381 If you miss the moment, you will walk away with the unambiguous sensation that you have not lived.

382 It's easier to complicate things than to simplify them.

383 A deep conviction is the product of shallow thinking.

384 A principle is a principle until it costs you money.

385 C'mon, make people laugh! He said. I'm in show business but I'm not a clown, I answered.

386 Melancholy means laziness dressed in a sophisticated way.

387 Those who give bad examples are the first offering good advice.

388 Love is always an afterthought; when we love someone we don't realise what we are doing.

389 With age I am not getting any wiser, just more careful.

390 I am full of contradictions and I never get bored: plenty to contemplate about myself.

391 I'd rather lose than cheat.

392 Some people have a clear conscience because they are empty inside.

She smiles like the sun as it breaks through the clouds.

393 You can say that you truly love someone only when you cannot say why.

394 Sometimes I feel like when it's raining heavily, there is nowhere to shelter.

395 She smiles like the sun as it breaks through the clouds.

396 I came to this world; I mean, I did not volunteer…

397 It's heart breaking to watch her struggle between what she actually wants and what she so desires.

398 I have a fading memory, which is why I'm sure I tattoo certain things on my brain.

399 I take pictures to stop time.

400 A glance reminds me at times how precious silence can be.

401 I don't want to get better; I enjoy my condition.

402 The most interesting people are always met in the most complicated circumstances.

403 She was smiling with tears in her heart.

404 She was always rebelling to be different, but so were all the others.

405 Don't ask me questions for which you are not prepared to hear the answer.

406 Live your life like a sculptor; take away the coarse and superfluous and gently chisel the fine details.

407 The self-confidence of the bully is fed by the indecision of the others.

408 While searching for perfection we destroy what was already good enough.

409 They keep remembering his wise and funny words. I will never forget his silences.

410 My stupidity is always comforting when I confront people who are too clever.

411 I have made many mistakes in my life; the biggest is that I haven't made enough of them.

412 I can't write today, I felt no love nor pain, just useless self-pity.

413 So many want to be right, while being truthful would be enough.

When I count the good things in life I always double the ones I did with you.

414 You shouldn't fear crying; tears will make you see better when your heart is too overwhelmed.

415 I received the best answers when I did not ask.

416 When I count the good things in life I always double the ones I did with you.

417 The secret of a successful life together is separate bathrooms.

418 There is always room for improvement, even when it feels crowded.

419 I dream alone at night and in good company during the day.

420 Today to be truly different you mustn't stand out.

421 As a parent there is only one certainty - you will always be wrong.

422 I don't want to have the ugly truth all the time; give me a beautiful lie from time to time.

423 When people smirk because I am different, I laugh because they are all the same.

424 Why is everyone is so worried about their reputation and not their conscience?

425 He was a life coach because his life was a game.

426 If someone suggests trying a different route, consider picking up the pace and finishing.

427 Some people live full speed with their hand-brake on.

428 When she couldn't understand, she would just make it up: that was the most dangerous thing.

429 Making sense of this world makes no sense at all.

430 It's a miracle, but like all miracles it will not last long enough.

431 We cannot wait for someone we do not know.

432 I don't have a bad character, just bad temperament.

433 My soul bears the scars of what my heart does.

434 I did not know that it would be the last time I was going to see her, because there is never a last time in our minds when we love someone.

I am not behaving strangely; it's you who cannot hear the music.

435 I don't mind if you quote me but I do mind if you quote me correctly.

436 At times, the best thing you can say is nothing at all.

437 I am not behaving strangely; it's you who cannot hear the music.

438 Some things make no sense because you are reading too much into them.

439 We see what we want to see when there is not much more to see.

440 I believe you and that is the problem - I believed you before.

441 Love, like a flame, needs something to burn otherwise there will be no fire.

442 Silence is golden because it will make you appear warm and bright.

443 Be scarce with the truth; don't lie but don't exaggerate either.

444 It cannot be useless if it's beautiful.

445 You know you love someone when hearing your name on their lips feels great.

446 My plan B is that there is no plan B.

447 Happiness only exists as moments; looking for constant happiness is a waste of time.

448 I wear my heart on my sleeve, tears and all.

449 He warmed up the desert night with a cup of coffee.

450 He complicates a simple task with ease, using the useless to make it difficult.

451 Say it once, but say it well.

452 I am not interested in giant steps in a grand direction; I enjoy small steps, bare feet in the snow.

453 I am full of defects like the holes on a flute; play me well and you'll like what I produce.

454 To forgive means to remember without suffering.

455 I am not *on* your side: I *am* your side.

456 There may be no wrong notes but it can still be out of tune.

My love for you is so strong that all the fish in the sea talk about it.

457 At times the best way to do it is to do it.

458 I love smelling your skin; I can savour how beautiful your soul is.

459 My love for you is so strong that all the fish in the sea talk about it.

460 We are always so scared to not be loved such that we forget to give love to those we scare.

461 Poetry is the most raped of all arts.

462 I have been so close to some people yet they did not see me.

463 The truth very rarely sits outside just waiting for us.

464 Truth hurts, but a lie can finish you off.

465 At times I get lost in my own thoughts, a world of dreams badly polluted by reality.

466 When I draw I don't *try* to draw, it just happens.

467 There is nothing more false than someone starting a sentence with 'to be honest'.

468 All the painful moments dig deep inside you; use that empty extra space and fill it with more joyful moments.

469 You'll have to tell the truth sooner or later, you can whisper it if you wish, but you must tell.

470 Push or pull, but get out of here.

471 I never touch the brakes; I always scrape on the sides, trying to slow myself down.

472 Everyone can incur debts when they have no money, but some manage when having plenty.

473 I prefer to be told that I'm crazy rather than insane.

474 I was really broken, in pieces so sharp that while picking myself up I was hurt even more.

475 I feel sorry for my guardian angel; nobody has ever been busier.

476 We love a film where people fall in love in unachievable ways.

477 Until you woke up I thought you were perfect.

478 Every time she spoke, the beautiful perception I had of her was contradicted.

I dream to rest my mind from too much reality.

479 I won't worry until the day I have no stories to tell.

480 I have no idea where people go once they die, but I do know where the ones dear to me remain.

481 I dream to rest my mind from too much reality.

482 One cannot be creative by accepting things as they are.

483 I am not scared of the Devil; I have met men who were far more evil.

484 I prefer a total lie to a half-truth.

485 A question of life or death: whose life for whose death?

486 Don't be afraid to show your weakness, even
if others make it their strength.

487 No point drowning your sorrows, they swim
perfectly well.

488 He who can truly talk doesn't make himself
noticed but remembered.

489 Nothing wrong with tears: like the sea, they
taste of depths few people can reach.

490 If we keep meeting each other like this, we
should at least exchange hugs.

491 I don't have a heart of stone - it beats too fast.

492 Like a child he is forever asking questions, but
unlike a child he does not accept the answers.

493 Today's heroes are made from solid trash.

494 "I have never forgotten you" hurts me much more than "Forget me".

495 Every lie contains a hidden truth.

496 The purpose of our dreams is to balance the reality we can't manage.

497 You don't want your heart to think, but you should think with your heart.

498 I want you to miss me when you are busy, surrounded by people, and with no time to think.

499 Some people take your work to pieces because they cannot face your integrity.

You don't have to leave; you can rest on my heart tonight.

500 People feel lonely because they are their own bad company.

501 Silence is the most comfortable place to be.

502 You don't have to leave; you can rest on my heart tonight.

503 We worry about the years of our life when it is the life in those years that we should worry about.

504 I don't always answer the phone; it doesn't have the right to be answered *whenever* it rings.

505 I have made lots of mistakes, but I have no regrets.

506 A pessimist is an optimist with real experience.

507 I always laugh myself silly in the company of intelligent people.

508 Why should an animal's suffering be different from ours? Have you ever looked in the eyes of a horse when it is hurt?

509 I believe in God but I mistrust his servants.

510 He was at war with the world; shame he did not notice the world was on his side.

511 I prefer the National Gallery to The Louvre as it is like visiting someone who has a beautiful collection; the Louvre is like someone fancying himself for his own art.

512 A conversation turns heavy in direct proportion to the lightness of the heads of the people involved.

513 I feel selfishly good with you because I make you feel good.

514 I've found it! I've found it! I cannot remember what it was but I have found it.

515 If you think you really love someone, you've just not loved enough.

516 Of course I am happy, it's just that I am in a hurry.

517 My brain always throws my heart ahead, and when successful, takes the credit for it.

518 You are worth what you look for.

519 A spontaneous act of kindness has the most casual beauty.

I was sitting in a corner of your notes, waiting to be read by your heart.

520 She was touching his hand, lips sealed, eyes closed, so many words shy of ruining that moment.

521 I treasure my losses more than I savour my achievements.

522 I was sitting in a corner of your notes, waiting to be read by your heart.

523 Only Hemingway could write beautifully while drunk, for he would then edit while sober.

524 Good writing is like the skill of a knife thrower, avoiding the target with great grace and precision while giving a great show.

525 I hate to repeat myself only because I don't like the sound of my own words.

526 I have some weird dreams; so weird that I often ask myself in the dream why I am dreaming such weird stuff.

527 She smelled wonderful, but not like a model from a catwalk or a famous actress; she smelled of home.

528 I don't mind being by myself, but I am scared of being alone.

529 I can cope with you not liking what I say, but couldn't bear it if you didn't understand my silence.

530 There is nothing bad with repeating yourself if the first time was good.

531 She has more plastic on her than my credit card.

532 I am a pessimist, because if I were an optimist I'd have no reason to want to change my future.

533 I suddenly felt that all that silly happiness made me sad.

534 If you really want to understand someone, observe how he laughs.

535 I'd rather hear a lie than be left in doubt.

536 When she holds my hand I feel like I am sand in an hourglass.

537 Don't sit on the fence, especially if there is nowhere to sit.

538 She was burning with fever, eyes filled with affliction, but she melted my cheek with her lips like the sun kissing snow.

I did not just fall in love: I lost all balance forever.

539 Failure sometimes is just the failure of not trying hard enough.

540 I am happy to trust my brain about what to avoid, but I prefer my heart in deciding what to pursue.

541 I did not just fall in love: I lost all balance forever.

542 No point looking for happiness, since happiness will find us if we deserve it.

543 Look forward always, even if your heart is lagging behind.

544 Today's 'Now!' is already too late since I had no answer to yesterday's 'When?'

545 We only live once, make sure it's enough.

546 Don't love someone and expect to change what you don't like in them; think of all the things you hate the most and if you still love them then it is true love.

547 What saddens me is that the wind will no longer play with me once I've lost my hair.

548 I don't want to get real - in fact, I don't get it at all this thing you call reality.

549 Be quiet, like a cat about to pounce on a bird.

550 When I was young and handsome, girls did not want to come to the cinema with me because I actually wanted to watch the movie.

551 The more I meet people of great intelligence the more I prefer people of great kindness.

552 Dog is man's best friend, but if man carries on like this, it will end up his only friend.

553 Anyone who says that they don't believe in love hasn't suffered enough.

554 Words give colour to the images I cannot imagine.

555 I welcome criticism - I just don't like critics.

556 There are people happy to explain life lessons they have never received, sharing experiences they never had.

557 He doesn't feel shame because he has no dignity.

558 I am not trying to be better than anyone else; I just want to improve all the time.

Music is a powerful eraser or a fabulous reminder.

118

559 His modesty is just a form of constipated pride.

560 I am what I read.

561 Music is a powerful eraser or a fabulous reminder.

562 Accept the things you cannot change and dare to change the things you can, but be wise enough to know the difference.

563 Freedom is letting your soul breathe deeply.

564 When we cry so much that we can't talk anymore it's because our words have sunk to the bottom of our heart.

565 Next time you feel embarrassed don't look at your feet, but look up to the sky.

566 I prefer tears in my eyes than blood on my hands.

567 A perfectionist who never completes is as bad as someone who attempts nothing.

568 The more he tries to come across as respectable, the more ridiculous he appears.

569 Life always has an answer to everything; it's your fault if you cannot read it.

570 Is he a genius? Really? For how long?

571 I love you sounds wonderful in every language but German.

572 I have returned from places where nobody is invited and from where nobody leaves.

573 Well, you can certainly do it *again*, but you could never come up with it in the first place.

574 Sorry, next time I'll make a better mistake.

575 She is always miserable; she must have won the 'who laughs first loses' game, every time since birth.

576 Only a dreamer can truly achieve something real.

577 The first quality you must have to speak well is to be able to listen carefully.

578 You can call yourself a man only when you push your own limits.

579 When it's raining, don't always look for cover, instead dance out in the open.

Try to hold your heart outside your body sometimes, it feels good.

580 I have never named a car or a camera in my life;
     I don't name anything that cannot respond.

581 I believed in atheism after I read Nietzsche.

582 Try to hold your heart outside your body some-
     times, it feels good.

583 Silence is golden but words can be cheap.

584 He understands so many books, but cannot
     read a single person.

585 We go out to look for things we have at home.

586 How can I feel bad about something that
     is a feeling? We can feel bad but cannot be
     bad because we feel.

587 A missed opportunity is a shot you did not take.

588 I don't strive to be happy; being content is already an achievement.

589 Live as though you are in a church with beautifully stained windows: when the sun is shining enjoy the show, but when it gets dark light some candles.

590 If you have an eye for it, you will appreciate what you love, without even looking.

591 You should never worry about what you don't know but instead about what you think you know.

592 You only realise that you are free once you move.

593 The pictures I love the most are the ones I cannot describe.

594 You can only know yourself once you've suffered.

595 I am not tough, not at all. I have met plenty of tough people and never had anything in common.

596 Smell is the most fragrant aphrodisiac.

597 He felt very important with his desk full of empty nothings.

598 The more you doubt, the less mistakes you make.

599 Words that fail to come are the ones bearing most truth.

600 Every time I opened myself to someone I froze to death.

Today's opportunists fly high sustained by their own hot air: the active passivity of vultures.

601 He was at the end but realized too late he'd had a bad beginning.

602 "Now" is a sharp axe that chops hours and throws them in the past with ruthless precision.

603 Today's opportunists fly high sustained by their own hot air: the active passivity of vultures.

604 We run in search of happiness and do not notice when we run right through it.

605 Some words never heal.

606 I never hide; everything is a front line in my life.

607 Some people I know change like a chameleon, dependent on what they happen upon.

608 Something always remains afterwards, even when nothing happened, because that nothing was something that did not happen.

609 You haven't lived until you make someone laugh.

610 As an engineer he was a disaster; he would build a dam from bridge drawings.

611 There are people who wait all their life to be chosen and who fail to choose.

612 Time is like space and money, there's never enough.

613 Nobody can understand what I did not do.

614 If you cry in the rain nobody will notice.

615 You cannot be brave unless you feel scared.

616 Try doing it *yourself* first; if you get help today you will expect it again tomorrow.

617 Is a perfect circle also a vicious cycle?

618 I am happy to be called lazy if I don't do what shouldn't be done.

619 The only thing I am always sure of is that I am always full of doubts.

620 We start free but end up caught in the chains we make.

621 I don't like to talk about my past, when described in words it loses all its glamour.

622 It's easy to not lie - just don't say anything.

Mine is not chaos, just an order that you don't understand.

623 I have no idea who I am most of the time, but there are plenty of people who happily tell me.

624 Success is always misunderstood and often overrated.

625 Mine is not chaos, just an order that you don't understand.

626 One can *see* beautiful things yet seldom *feel* beauty.

627 Worse than to not be loved is to be loved no more.

628 Why do you love me? He asked. Because whenever I see you I fall, and you are there to catch me.

629 I felt neither foreign, nor really quite at home.

630 She always spoke so fast, always downhill, without brakes or steering.

631 Obstinate honesty is just bad manners.

632 I contradict myself all the time; coherence is a synonym of conformity.

633 The problem with succeeding is that you have to keep doing it; with failure you don't have to.

634 Innovation comes from visionaries and bad men, not conformists or followers.

635 We might all be on the same boat but some don't seem to be rowing.

636 You can speak any language if you are hungry enough.

637 A moralist judges others, a person with morality judges himself.

638 We feel so powerful when we flatten an ant, but the real power is the ability to create one.

639 I learn more each time I say goodbye to someone I love.

640 Don't look at me with your eyes, look at me with your heart.

641 The life that you are not living is often the one worth living.

642 As a child, my invisible friend had more problems than I did.

643 I am very good at talking about 'my bad'.

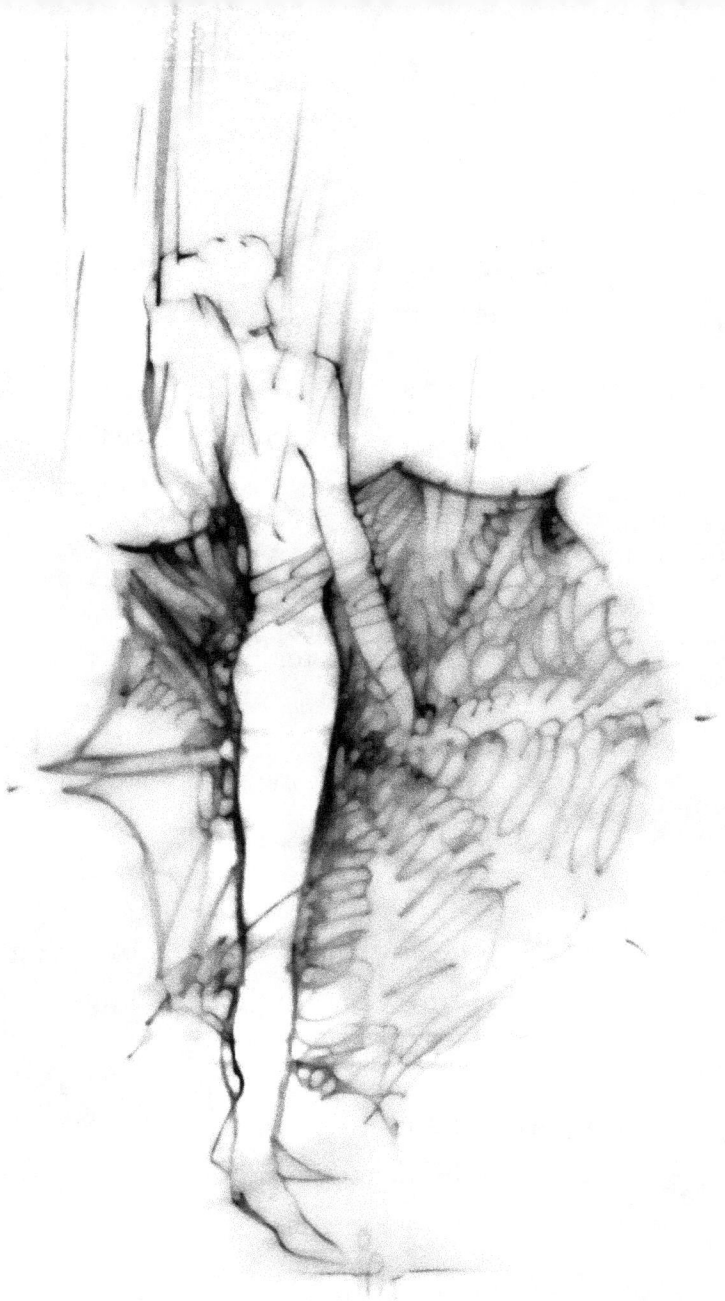

I hate umbrellas ... and love feeling the rain.

644 I have been in a house of butterflies; there were no walls, just colourful ever-changing wallpaper.

645 My defects make me perfect to be loved.

646 Missed opportunities never fail to kill me a little each time.

647 I hate umbrellas ... and love feeling the rain.

648 Not sure you are clever enough? Doubting it is already very clever.

649 In trying to be unique we end up all the same.

650 I might not know what I am doing but I always know where I am going.

651 Your enemy's worst moment is your finest.

652 'I could've done that' is the most irritating thing anyone can say.

653 Don't blame the circumstances, most of the time they are of your own doing.

654 Some people are like snowflakes: when you try to hold them they disappear, leaving a tear.

655 We should worry about how much others believe in us, not how much or what we believe.

656 The things you call dear cannot comfort you; they just consume you with memories, costing you tears and pain. That is why they are called dear.

657 Just remember to write I LOVE YOU in capital letters on your heart.

658 I have a low opinion of myself until I meet those who really know me.

659 Without you my life would be a mistake.

660 I'd rather be detested for what I truly am, than admired for what I falsely appear.

661 She is very good at sharing opinions she does not have.

662 You watch a movie but you dream a book.

663 Why do the right words always come at the wrong moment?

664 Fearing tomorrow spoils today.

665 He has a superiority complex sustained by hidden heels.

Embrace your demons to cuddle your angels.

666 Don't blind yourself and then say that the sun doesn't shine.

667 You are never really busy if you have time to stop and say you are.

668 Embrace your demons to cuddle your angels.

669 A creative mind takes no breaks, only short pauses.

670 The moral of the story is the same old story.

671 If you aim low, you will never be disappointed, but you will always wonder what you could have achieved aiming higher.

672 Too deep into the argument and you might drown.

673 Thank you for the fun; even when it wasn't.

674 Maybe I *am* crazy, but if you are sane I think people would rather have *you* in a straight jacket.

675 Instead of pointing out what is wrong, show me how to do it right.

676 Doing good might end up badly – only you can decide if it's worth it.

677 He fancies himself as a big cheese but he is just a grated stinker.

678 My thoughts are beautifully written, but badly translated.

679 Reality owes me things my dreams cannot afford.

680 I'd rather be in danger from an act of bravery than be safe from an act of cowardice.

681 It's never nobody's fault.

682 Some people bury their head in the sand, but when they surface it's not sand they are covered with; the smell gives it away.

683 If you are feeling sorry for yourself it means you are not busy enough.

684 I listen in the dark and talk in the sun.

685 The most upsetting thing for people who don't like you is for them to see you happy.

686 A half-truth told with ill intentions is worse than a complete lie.

Send your lips to a new address, I have moved.

687 I upset my bank manager when I told her I keep my account in the red to keep the bank in profit.

688 What is the point of being able to afford expensive watches and then have no time for anything?

689 Send your lips to a new address, I have moved.

690 You don't have to say everything you think but you'd better think about what you're going to say.

691 The best way to be in good faith is to admit that you can't be.

692 I felt like shells on the beach, rolled over by waves on the wet sand.

693 When lighting, you don't create: you discover.

694 As a freelancer I don't have holidays, just coffee breaks.

695 A relationship is between three parties: you, me and us.

696 Always speak your words with a sprinkling of sugar on top; you might have to eat them tomorrow.

697 Say it with flowers but underline it with chocolates.

698 I never try to understand, I just want to know.

699 Some people dwell in a past that they do not have.

700 I am a daydreamer because I am a nightcrawler.

701 Common sense makes no sense to him.

702 Every time I dialled the wrong number someone always answered.

703 I don't stay up on New Year 's Eve anymore, it comes later and later each year.

704 After seeing the Uffizi museum in Florence I
realised one life is definitely not enough.

705 Time and silence cannot be bought, nor
negotiated.

706 They say that nothing is impossible if you
really want it. That sounds implausible to me.

707 When you close your eyes to rest, let me know
so you're there when I close mine.

When she talks she moves her head like a snake preparing for the bite.

708 You will not be disappointed if you don't have delusional expectations.

709 His false modesty is easily exposed by his true arrogance.

710 When she talks she moves her head like a snake preparing for the bite.

711 He always tells everyone what he has done, but it's hard to understand who he is.

712 A half-truth becomes a full lie if not left alone.

713 I leave envy to people who always think what they should have had instead of what they have.

714 I write because I am terrified of being forgotten, even though I often end up writing forgettable things.

715 I live an expensive life; I pay dearly for many choices.

716 I am always weary of anyone who uses too many words to express something.

717 Dream big and build those dreams.

718 Her ideal *real man* is a perfectly waxed, anorexic, effeminate nymph.

719 I don't want to write anything clever, I wouldn't be able to replicate it.

720 I have burned some bridges and enjoyed the show.

721 I don't like staring at dumb clouds; I'd rather watch ants in the grass, intelligently busy.

722 Say one thing and say it well if you want it to be remembered.

723 He is vague to the point of meaningless.

724 If you have nothing to do, take your nothing elsewhere.

725 Peace comes in your mind when expectation leaves.

726 His head is so full of rubbish that there is no more space for anything else.

727 Where there is a will there is a way, but never the other way around.

728 Yes, I have the answer, albeit a different one of you ask me tomorrow.

Weird how I end up in places so rarely by choice.

729 Every time I got it wrong I discovered something right about myself.

730 I am not a 'landscape of sentiments' tour guide.

731 We buy things we can't afford to sustain a life
we do not need.

732 Weird how I end up in places so rarely by
choice.

733 There is far more reality than anyone can ever
dream.

734 No big change can happen without some small
painful change alongside it.

735 A boat cannot sink unless water gets inside, so
don't allow bad feelings inside, and keep
paddling.

736 What happened to what you learned at school? Did you unload it as fast as dead-weight?

737 Never work for people who stand for nothing.

738 He is worse than a liar: he tells me my own stories as if they were his own.

739 I disappoint myself when I am right.

740 Chronological order sounds like a terrible disease.

741 A pessimist is someone who has been overexposed to way too many people yearning for happiness.

742 A real craftsman never blames his fools.

743 Talent is nurtured by action; I have never heard of someone with great talent doing nothing all day.

744 I often feel lost, with a strong sense of direction.

745 It's never a question of who is right, but who is left.

746 I don't understand 'killing time', since Time has the volume deal with the obituary.

747 I like the wind; it impertinently manages to clean or cloud our vision with a bout of whim.

748 What is the point of brushing teeth after a coffee? You might as well have a cup of toothpaste.

Sweat over small things, they might lead to bigger things.

749 I don't try to defend what I believe, but to be what I defend.

750 He set up a meeting to plan the meetings for the week.

751 Silence is the space where the mind can find some dialogue.

752 Sweat over small things, they might lead to bigger things.

753 Not everyone can start a revolution, but we can all try an evolution every now and then.

754 I would hate to be called an artist, but instead prefer to be known as a craftsman.

755 A picture that tells all is worse than someone explaining the picture.

756 I never noticed his presence but I miss his absence.

757 I started writing in my youth because we couldn't afford to travel.

758 It is not true that I don't have a sense of direction; I do, but it's the wrong one!

759 Why ask me which camera I use? Does anyone want to know which brush a painter chose?

760 Old age is not something to die for.

761 As a child I was an endangered species, always exposing myself to danger.

762 I was never comfortable with anyone who has memories filed in good order.

763 I didn't finish reading the Bible; my friends spoiled it by telling me that the Devil did it.

764 The more images you watch, the better photos you'll take; like reading with writing.

765 Living in hope is worse than a moment of disappointment.

766 He fancies himself as a new Messiah, disciples and all.

767 Dying for a cause isn't much of a living.

768 A cynic wonders whether this phrase is intentionally rubbish, while a pessimist wonders whether there is any hope of improving it.

769 Hype is a perverse tool to create plastic fantasies.

Seduction is not an attitude but an appetite.

770 You should never compare your life to others', since you don't know what compromises they had to make.

771 There is an old saying in the film industry: action!

772 Seduction is not an attitude but an appetite.

773 Inspirational quotes are easy to read but tough to follow.

774 I think she has a 'blonde' complex.

775 It is pointless to pretend you agree; your eyes will not buy into it.

776 You can see the advantages of pessimism only if you are a true optimist.

777 I am never surprised at the intelligence of an animal or the stupidity of man.

778 There are never perfect conditions in the beginning, but to actually make a start is the ideal way forward.

779 Once upon a time there was no more time.

780 Even if you don't believe in a God or anything, it's a great feeling when someone believes in you.

781 He wasn't capable of being available to be dependable with his ability.

782 To get to where you want there are no shortcuts, just a hard walk.

783 I didn't have a dad, but a father, belt and all.

784 Happiness is not a state of mind but just a moment in which we touch something extraordinary; if it lasts too long, we'd go insane.

785 The more he talked the more I realised he had nothing to say.

786 She kept saying that she wished her dog could talk. Looking at the dog it was clear he wished that *she* would shut up.

787 Italians are obsessed with conspiracy theories; I am pretty sure there must be someone behind that.

788 Don't be ashamed for failing often, but shame on you for not trying often enough.

789 If it doesn't work, take a few side steps and look again from a different angle.

An animal is the beast teacher for our kids.

790 He has many qualities, I cannot recall any of them now, but he will list them himself when you meet him.

791 I have met plenty of dreamers with a better reality.

792 An animal is the beast teacher for our kids.

793 My mum used to call me by our dog's name. When I complained she replied that the dog didn't mind.

794 It's never a good time, but it's always time to be good.

795 I don't try to impress, just to express.

796 That seems reasonable to me, the voice of reason doesn't speak reason!

797 The movie industry is mainly driven today by short-sighted producers looking for shortcuts where pros are short-changed for short-term gain.

798 As I grow old nothing changes but the dosage.

799 My memory is constantly blown up by the anarchy of sentiments.

800 You can quote me on that, anonymously.

801 A father is a great teacher but a terrible instructor.

802 So many talk so much talk but with so little to say.

803 I never wear armour, you can tell by the many scars I have.

804 I will take him as is, ego and all; and treat him accordingly.

805 Don't take the present for granted - it is not a gift.

806 With all those personality issues, he needs a magazine rack to file them in good order.

807 Listening isn't just about words spoken, but the ones swallowed too.

808 My grandfather was a man of few words ... all of which were hard to understand.

809 It is politically incorrect and no amount of correction can correct that.

810 Title something with '...', and let other people fill in with words.

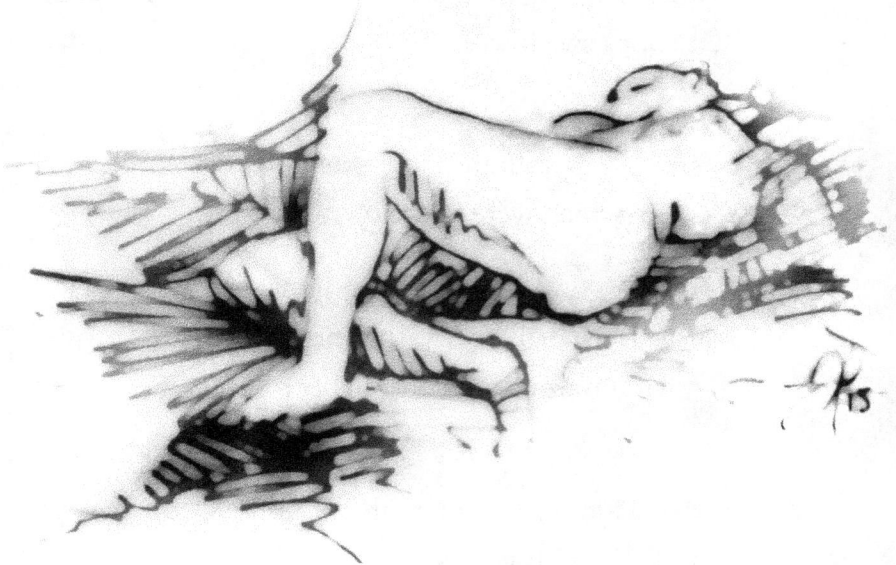

Why do we say 'falling in love'? Is it because we get hurt afterwards?

811 If you don't value yourself then nobody else will.

812 Some people become home to me.

813 I am often on my own because I am always on time.

814 Why do we say 'falling in love'? Is it because we get hurt afterwards?

815 Italy is a country where the provisional becomes institutionalized.

816 For sure I have a head full of doubts, which questions this one certainty.

817 I collect words thrown away by others, to say what they were keeping for themselves.

818 It's hard to keep watch over my heart as my mind randomly yet constantly wanders.

819 We look for alien life without realising it might be us.

820 We must give what it has cost us to be worthy of receiving.

821 It's the thought that counts but the gesture that matters.

822 My creativity is like a tide pulled by a capricious moon.

823 We can't always be clouds, we should turn into rain when necessary.

824 A luminous smile reflects the colours of a beautiful mind.

825 Don't underestimate the creativity of others while training your own.

826 I am a dreamer because reality is vastly overrated.

827 Trust me, I am Italian.

828 I ignored some terrible advice and made some excellent mistakes.

829 A book doesn't end, but lives in words.

Franz Pagot on set in Malta.

About the Author

Franz Pagot was born near Venice, Italy, and was educated in the classics. His celluloid addiction took him to Milan, where he worked on all kinds of jobs to support his habit - filming advertisements, animations and the odd documentary. In 1989 he moved to London, ultimately establishing himself as a cinematographer in feature films and TV commercials. He is a BAFTA member and has won many international awards. He lives in London.